What Was It Like?™
HARRIET TUBMAN

by Jane Polcovar
illustrated by Alex Bloch

CHILDRENS PRESS CHOICE

A Longmeadow title selected for educational distribution

ISBN 0-516-09554-4

Even though there are many tall tales about me, the truth is I never did get to be very tall. I just about reached five feet when I was all grown up. But one thing I was never short on was names. I was called by three different names at different times in my life. I guess I grew into each one of them in its own time.

I was born in a windowless cabin in the slave quarters of a big plantation on the Maryland shore. The owner of the plantation, our master, lived in a big house not far from us. Friends of my parents came by to admire me, though it worried them somewhat that I was a girl, instead of a boy. They christened me Araminta, but called me Minty.

To my parents, I was a gift from God even if I wasn't a boy. But everyone knew that girls weren't worth as much to the master since we couldn't do as much woodchopping. And if the master felt like it, he might just sell one of those girl children to a cotton plantation further south. So I wouldn't be surprised if somebody hoped out loud that my folks could maybe find a way to get me trained as a cook, or a weaver, or a white child's nurse. That would give me a better chance of staying with them. Lots of parents before mine had already watched with tears in their eyes as their children were taken away from them. Their

2

Otto

little ones pulled against their chains and cried out for help, but there was nothing they could do.

My mother's name was Harriet Greene, though most people called her Old Rit. And my father's name was Benjamin Ross. They were the property of Edward Brodas and lived on his plantation in Maryland. From the first moment I opened my eyes (that was in 1821), I also was Mr. Brodas's property—just like one of his horses. Even though my Mama cradled me in her arms and my Papa sang to me, it was the master—Mr. Brodas—to whom I belonged.

My folks worked in the fields along with the other slaves. They started when the sun rose, and didn't stop until it went down again. Naturally they didn't have much time to be with me. So until I was about five years old, I had to stay with the other small children while an old woman watched over us. She couldn't work in the fields anymore, but that didn't mean she was too old to take a switch to us if we strayed too far or didn't do as she said.

I loved it when she told us stories. We'd all sit around her, wide-eyed, as she talked about our ancestors, the free blacks. They were people who were stolen from Africa and stuffed together by the hundreds into the hold of a great ship. They were kings and medicine men, great warriors and teachers who were taken to a strange land far across the ocean. There they were put on auction blocks where their teeth and their muscles were poked and examined and people would decide how much they wanted to pay to own them. Then the slaves were led away in chains. Children were often separated forever from their mothers, brothers from their sisters, husbands from their wives.

She told stories, too, about brave slaves who had tried to get away from their masters. There was a kind of freedom line that ran across the state boundary line between Maryland and Pennsylvania. If you could run and hide well enough, you could manage to get away from the slave catchers who would try to hunt you down. And then if you could somehow get far enough north without starving or freezing or getting lost on the way, you'd be free!

Even at my age, I knew of some runaways who had been brought back. Sometimes at night we'd hear the hoofbeats of the white overseers' horses as they pounded through the slave quarters, dragging a beaten runaway behind them. They'd cut the rope and leave his bleeding body in a heap outside the cabins.

When I was six years old, my days of being cared for were over. I was sent into the fields to carry water buckets to the workers. I didn't really mind, because then I got to see my folks bending over the corn, and I could listen to all the field slaves singing. They sang to make their work go more easily, but they also sang because the overseer, watching with his whip in his hand, didn't like it when the slaves were quiet. The silence might mean we were thinking about escaping. He didn't like talking, either, because that might mean we were planning an escape. But when we sang, he told the master we were happy.

What the man didn't know was that when we sang, our songs were to remind us about freedom, and about God, and to keep up our hopes for a better day. He didn't know because when he came near we sometimes sang nonsense, so he stopped listening carefully to the words. It was also because we used words that hid what we were really singing about. Maybe our English didn't sound like white folks', but that could just be because a slave wasn't allowed to get an education! The fact is, if I had ever been caught looking into a book—if I could somehow have gotten hold of one—so as to teach myself reading and writing, I would have gotten whipped for being "uppity."

But our words were full of meaning for us. Even when we hid the message, we all knew what it meant when we sang:

> *Go down, Moses,*
> *Way down in Egypt's land*
> *Tell Old Pharaoh*
> *Let my people go.*

The song was about Moses from the Bible, and how he brought his people from slavery into freedom. It made us feel better to sing freedom songs right under the overseer's nose, without him ever catching on. If we could sing about freedom, it meant that there was hope.

One day as I came back from bringing water to the field hands, one of my master's house slaves came running up to me, out of breath. He had just heard a white woman telling Mr. Brodas that she wanted to hire a little girl slave for whom she would only have to pay a few pennies a week.

Before I knew what was happening, a woman came for me in a buckboard. When I started to cry, the woman told me to keep quiet or she'd hit me.

She didn't say another word to me during the long ride to her home which turned out to be run-down, and much smaller than the master's house. As we went inside, I kept thinking of my Mama and Papa and wondering if they'd even be told about what had happened to me. The woman told me to call her Miss Susan. She said that my job was to clean her house and make sure that her baby never cried. She handed me a cloth and said, "Show me how you dust the furniture. You'd better do a good job, you hear?"

Every night I sat on her bedroom floor near the cradle, ready to rock it the moment the baby started to cry. If I dozed off or didn't pick up the baby quickly enough, Miss Susan got that whip down from the shelf again. After a while, I got so that I could sleep for a few minutes at a time and still manage to hear the baby's first wail. Even so, the scars I got from those whippings stayed with me for the rest of my life.

One day, as I stood behind a chair waiting for Miss Susan to hand me the baby, I saw a dish of sugar on the kitchen table. I had never tasted sugar. When I thought she wasn't looking, I slowly reached out to take some. But she turned just then and saw me, and grabbed for her whip. I ran straight out of the house and kept on going.

But where was I running to? I had no idea. I hid for five days and nights behind a pig pen, eating scraps that were meant for the animals. Finally, when I couldn't take it anymore, I went back. Miss Susan returned me to my master and told him that I wasn't worth the six pennies a week she was paying for me.

I was home now! But not for long. I was hired out again a few months later to another family. Mr. Cook was a trapper, and his wife was a weaver. My folks thought that this might be a lucky thing because if I learned to weave, the master might think I was too useful to sell down the river.

I tried to learn how to weave, but I had trouble with it. My fingers were too rough from all the outdoor work I had done. The thin thread kept getting tangled in my fingers. I also coughed a lot from the tiny bits of wool that were always floating in the air.

Mr. Cook said, "Let me have her. She can help me set bait for the muskrats and check the traps."

At first I was glad to be out of that house. But then the weather turned cold. I had to wade into freezing creeks and marshes, so my clothes were always wet. One morning I woke from my sleeping place on the floor shaking with fever. Mrs. Cook told her husband that it was an old slave

trick to pretend to be sick in order to get out of working. She said that even at seven years old I must have learned it already. So he sent me out to his traps, anyway.

When I stumbled back to the house that night burning hot, they saw that I really *was* sick. I was so sick they thought I might even die. Mr. Cook didn't want that to happen in his house, so he brought me back to my Mama and Papa. It felt so good to be taken care of!

Slowly I got better. But the sickness had done something to my voice. It was always very husky after that. There was one good thing about that. When I sang, everybody knew that it was me.

When the overseer said that I was well enough, he put me to work in the fields alongside the grown-ups. At night, when we were all sitting around the cabins, I'd listen to them telling stories. One of my favorite stories was about a master who was chasing an escaping slave. He had almost caught up with him when the runaway disappeared. The master looked for hours, but it was as if the boy had vanished on an underground road. They say that the Underground Railroad got its name from that story.

Now, the Underground Railroad wasn't really

underground and it wasn't really a railroad. It was a name given to an organization of some white people who hated slavery and some free blacks. They were mostly from the North, and they'd secretly risk their lives to help slaves escape to freedom. There were what they called "stations" on this railroad, which were really hideouts. These were people's homes and barns and haylofts where runaways would be hidden, then fed and protected until they could be sent on to the next station when it was safer to travel. Some homes had tunnels dug under the floorboards which went underneath the house and came up again a few hundred feet away in the shelter of the woods nearby. That way no one would be seen entering or leaving. But most stations on the Underground Railroad were just ordinary homes or barns, with very special people willing to risk their safety to help others. The runaways would be sent on to the next "stop," and the next, until they had crossed into the North and freedom.

These stories made me tingle. They gave me hope. Someday, no person would own another! Someday, we'd all be free!

One day, when I was loading a wagon, I saw a slave hand, maybe fifteen years old, drop his ax

and race like the wind across the field. The overseer took off right after him, yelling at him to stop
or he would kill him. I got so frightened for the boy
that I dropped my armload of wood and followed
the two of them all the way to town. By the time I
caught up with them, the boy had run into a store.
The overseer was standing over him, looking like
he was ready to do what he had threatened. Then
he saw me outside and ordered me to help him tie
the boy's hands, so that he could whip him.

I didn't move.

The slave saw his chance, jumped to his feet and
ran out right past me. I stepped into the doorway,
hoping to give the boy an extra few seconds to get
away. The overseer got so angry that he grabbed a
heavy iron weight and hurled it after the runaway. It crashed into my head, throwing me back-
ward to the floor. He scooped me up and brought
me to my cabin, calmly telling my Papa that I
probably wouldn't live through the night.

I don't remember much of the next eight
months, but I'm told that everyone was sure I was
going to die. They said that no one could live with
his head smashed like mine had been. I slept for
most of the next year. My folks fed me, and tended
me. They knew that if I lived, I'd be sold south.
Master didn't want any slave who wouldn't listen.

So they figured, live or die, I'd be taken away from them, forever.

Finally, the deep scar on my forehead began to heal, and I was sent into the fields once more. But I knew for sure that things had changed. Even the older people would come over to me, asking what I thought of this or that. And when I had an idea about something, everyone would listen. After all, I had done a very grown-up thing. I had put someone else's needs ahead of my own. Soon everyone started calling me Harriet. I wasn't Minty anymore. I was no longer a child.

Not long afterward, my life was turned upside down again because the master died suddenly. Until his kinfolk decided what to do with his possessions—which included all of his slaves— they hired out my father and me to a man named John Stewart. Papa was sent to work in the nearby forest chopping trees. I was put in the kitchen of Mr. Stewart's house to clean and cook. After many months I got up my courage and asked if I could be allowed to work in the woods with the men.

"You?" he laughed, studying his tiny kitchen slave. "Don't be ridiculous." I reminded him politely that female slaves were so much cheaper to buy. If he could get a man's work from a woman slave, he'd be getting a bargain. He agreed with me there, and with a grin on his face he said, "Why not?"

I was cutting those trees as fast as anyone, and even faster than many of the bigger men. I could load the timbers onto the wagons easily, too. After all, I had been loading wood day in and day out at Edward Brodas's plantation. So it didn't surprise me that this work wasn't hard.

But it sure surprised Mr. Stewart!

I never did have to go back into his kitchen. I liked that, but I hated it when he showed me off to his friends. He'd give orders to have me hitched to a flatboat loaded with stones. They'd watch from their fancy porch, laughing and applauding as I walked along the edge of the river, the boat dragging behind me just as if I were a plow horse!

John Stewart's gentlemen weren't the only ones who pointed and stared when he made me do that. Many of the field hands would glance up from their work to watch, too. But I didn't mind that. They were looking with kind eyes, the way people who spend their days using their bodies do. I'd try to spot John Tubman in the field, to see if he was looking my way. Sometimes, I'd catch him watching me as I worked. And I was glad because he had an easy, quick laugh and he was tall and handsome.

John Tubman was different from any man I'd ever known. And well he should be, because he was a *free* black man. He had never been any man's slave. His folks were freed by their master after many years, and John had been born free. He hired himself out, and he could keep the money he made. This free man with the sparkling eyes was taken with me — a slave woman!

I was the happiest I'd ever been in my life when, a short while later, we were married. I moved into his cabin at the edge of the plantation, eager for my new life as Mrs. Harriet Tubman.

Even though I was very happy, I still kept dreaming of being free. My best days were clouded by the feeling that my life wasn't my own, and that I could be taken away from my husband at any time. But whenever I'd share these thoughts with John, he'd get upset.

Maybe because he was free he couldn't understand what it was like for me to be owned by a master. For a while, I thought he was afraid that if we ran off and got caught, they would take us away from each other. Or maybe he was just afraid of being punished for putting such thoughts in my head. Whatever it was, he got so angry whenever I even spoke about it, that I had to stop telling him how I felt. But that wish in my heart never went away.

Six years went by—years filled with chopping trees, and with swinging an ax beside my father and my husband. But they were six years of being a slave, too. One good thing came out of Mr. Stewart's taking a liking to my work. After a while, he let me hire myself out. I had to give him a dollar a week, but anything I earned over that I could keep. It was my first chance to have money of my very own! I looked for out-of-door jobs plowing fields, hauling logs—anything I could do when my regular day's work was done.

After close to a year of working day and night, I had twenty dollars saved. I wrapped it all in a piece of cloth. Then I went to my master and asked him how much it would cost to buy my freedom.

When I showed him what was in the cloth, he burst out laughing. "Come back," he said, "when you've got five hundred good American dollars in your hand to show me. Then we'll talk about your freedom."

Now, where in the world was I ever going to get so much money? There was just no way, no way at all to be free, unless I ran away! It wasn't long afterwards—while I was thinking about that very thing—when I learned that all of the slaves were going to be sold to some cotton plantations down south. Edward Brodas's family had finally decided what to do with all of his property—they were selling it all off! A few days later two of my sisters were sent away, and it broke my heart.

That night, when John was fast asleep, I went to the slave quarters and talked three of my brothers into running north with me. I led the way through the woods, which I knew pretty well. It was dark, and the moon was hidden by clouds so we couldn't see a thing. We stumbled over thick tree roots, and our legs were scratched by burrs and brambles. We jumped at every sound, thinking the slave catchers were right behind us with their horses and their guns. After about an hour my brothers stopped and said they were too afraid to go on. They were sure we were going to be captured and killed. I pleaded with them not to turn back, but they wouldn't listen. They wouldn't even let me

go by myself. I was dragged back to the plantation. When I slipped silently into the cabin, I found John still fast asleep. He'd never even known I was gone.

I was working under the hot sun in the fields a few days later when I saw the water boy heading my way with his bucket. As I bent down to get a drink, he whispered in my ear, "Master sold you. You'll be off with a chain gang tomorrow." Then he hurried off, and I went back to work. I was shaken and I was scared, but I knew what I had to do.

This time I didn't tell a soul about it—not even my Mama and my Papa. I ached to hold them in my arms for the last time, but if later on the master even thought that my folks knew something about my escape, they'd be severely punished. But I wanted to leave them some kind of message. So just before I slipped away from the plantation, I went past the big house where one of my sisters worked. Then I sang in my husky voice:

> *When that old chariot comes,*
> *I'm going to leave you.*
> *I'm bound for the Promised Land,*
> *Friends, I'm going to leave you.*

I hoped that after I was gone she would remember hearing my song and would tell our folks that

I had tried to say goodbye.

I packed the extra bits of salt pork I had saved over the weeks in an old cloth. That, and berries from the woods, would be my food for a while. Then I waited until John's snores filled the cabin, and I was gone!

I had to be quiet in the woods. I also had to move as fast as I could. Hunters would be searching for me by morning. If they found me, they would kill me for sure! It was a good reason to keep running, but I was as scared as could be. All night long I had to keep reminding myself, "I am the Lord's child. And I have a right to be free."

The first place I headed for was a nearby town called Bucktown, and the home of a certain white woman. From the time I was little I had heard stories about a group of people called Quakers. They called themselves the Society of Friends, and friends are just what they were to slaves. These white people spoke as if they were reading from the Bible, dressed in plain gray or black clothes, and believed with all their hearts that slavery was evil. Not only that, but they did something about it!

Now I was going to the home of a Quaker woman who had stopped her buggy once a long time ago to ask me how I had gotten the scar on my forehead. When I told her, she said that if I ever needed a safe place to go, she wanted me to know where she lived. And I had remembered her directions!

I crept up to her house by daybreak, looked around and didn't see anyone. Softly, I knocked on the door. She opened it, and didn't even seem surprised to see me. She took me to a back room and fed me. Then she told me not to worry. There were friends who would help me get from one station to another all along the railroad.

She left me alone to get some rest. Lying there, I thought about this wonderful white woman who was taking such chances to help a black slave. If they caught her, she would probably go to jail. Then they would take away everything she owned to make her pay for stealing a slave master's property. I said a little prayer for her and drifted off to sleep.

She woke me when it grew dark, then gave me a note that she had written to a Mr. John Hunn in a town in Delaware, which was to be my next stop. She told me which river to follow, and where I would find a certain road that would lead me to his farmhouse. "Follow the road," she said "but do not walk on it, lest you are spotted."

Before I left, I wanted to give her something to

show her how much I appreciated what she was doing for me. But I had nothing to offer, nothing but a simple, "Thank you, Ma'am." That seemed to do just fine. She broke into a smile that was like the morning sun. "Godspeed," she called out after me, as I headed back into the shelter of the forest.

I hurried all through the night, listening carefully for the sounds of horses coming. I knew slave hunters were out there by now, looking everywhere for me. But I had already spent one day and night away from the slave quarters—and away from a master who could beat me or sell me. That thought gave me hope!

I stumbled along until I could hardly feel my feet anymore. It was already daylight when I saw the house of John Hunn. By then, I really needed a safe place to rest! As I went around to the back door, a woman wearing a sunbonnet stepped into the early morning light. She stared at me for a moment. Then she quickly grabbed a broom and shoved it into my hand. "Sweep the porch!" she whispered, and then went back inside and closed the door.

I didn't know what was going on, but I began to sweep. Just then, a man came out of the house, waving goodbye to the folks who lived there. Suddenly, I understood. He didn't give me more than a glance before he went away. As soon as he left, I got a real welcome and something to eat.

That night, Mr. Hunn, who was a farmer, loaded some bushels of corn and potatoes onto his wagon. This was to be my cover, he told me with a smile. When I climbed in, he covered me with a blanket. Then some vegetables were spread over the blanket and I got myself a wagon ride! This time, I reminded myself, it wasn't in Miss Susan's buckboard, taking me away to get whippings for not keeping her baby quiet...or for trying to touch a lump of sugar.

Lying there under the blanket for so long with nothing to do, I began to have some strange ideas. Maybe Mr. Hunn had covered my face so that he could really take me back to the plantation! All of a sudden, we stopped and I felt the blanket being pulled away from me. "Come, I'll help you down," said Mr. Hunn. He gave me his hand, and then I felt badly for not trusting him. He pointed to a river that was off to the right of the road. "Follow it upstream," he said, and he told me what to look

for next. With a wave he turned his wagon around and was gone. I was left alone in the night.

Well, there were a lot of other stops, too, on my freedom walk. I was hidden in the attic of a Quaker home, in a German farmer's haystack and in a potato hole in the floor of a cabin that belonged to a free black family. I was rowed across a river by a man whose face I couldn't see in the darkness. And now, about a hundred miles from the plantation where I was born into slavery, I crossed the freedom line! In the state of Pennsylvania, no person could own another person, so I was finally free!

The sun was just coming up. I looked at my hands to see if I was the same person now that I was free. There was such a glory over everything! The sun shone like gold through the trees and over the fields and I felt like I was in Heaven.

But that feeling didn't last for very long before I began to realize that something was missing—the people I loved. There was no one to welcome me to this land of freedom. I was a stranger in a strange land. And that's how it would be until my Mama and my Papa and all my brothers and sisters could share this freedom with me. Someday soon I had to go back to Maryland. Then I would bring my family to the Promised Land!

But I needed a lot of help and I found it in a little office above a store. It was called the Philadelphia Vigilance Committee. A black man, William Still, and a white man, J. Miller McKim, were its secretary and president. This was where runaway slaves went to meet each other to see if they could find out news about their families.

It was here that I heard about Mary, one of my sisters, and her family. They had tried to escape, too, but they had only gotten as far as Baltimore, Maryland. They were still in slave territory, and they needed someone to help get them the rest of the way out. When I said that *I* would go, Mr. Still shook his head.

"You won't stand a chance. You're a runaway. They've got posters up for you that say 'Wanted— Dead or Alive!'"

"I still want to go," I said.

Then Mr. McKim shook his head. "Sorry, Harriet. We know you mean well. But the conductors we use on our Underground Railroad have always been men. There's a good reason for it, too—everybody would be suspicious of a woman traveling alone."

"Now listen," I said. "I've been doing a man's work all my life. Now I'll just have to dress like one."

When they saw that I was going, no matter what, they got tired of arguing with me. They gave me some advice and directions, shook hands with me and back I went into slave territory. Well, I found my sister and her family in one of our secret stations, a big farmhouse just outside Baltimore. But that man's disguise of mine worked so well that even my sister didn't recognize me until I started to sing to her. She sure knew that voice of mine! Mary burst out laughing and crying at the same time.

"Harriet! It's Harriet!" she yelled and rushed into my arms.

A few days later we set off for the next station stop on our journey north. It was winter. Heavy snow started falling. We walked mile after mile. Our feet grew numb and our shoes split open. Mary's two small children were a problem, too. We were moving in secret. What if one of them cried out at the wrong time and we were discovered by somebody who would turn us in?

The children had plenty to cry about, too, with the cold and the hunger and the fear we all had. I had to be brave because they were all looking up to me to get them through. I had to act like I'd done this before—which I hadn't—not with other people to be responsible for! But we all hung on. Those children didn't make a whimper, even when we had to huddle together in freezing swamp water—while just over our heads slave hunters were standing on a bridge with guns, looking for us.

The year was 1850. That was my first trip as a conductor on the Underground Railroad, but it wasn't my last. A few months later I rescued one of my brothers from a plantation in Maryland and brought two other slaves back to Philadelphia with him. Then a terrible law was passed to help slave owners get back their runaways from the free states in the North. Under the Fugitive Slave Law it became a crime to help a slave even if he had crossed the line into a state that didn't allow slavery! That meant that the people in Philadelphia who had helped us could go to jail.

Suddenly, handbills describing runaway slaves were put up on walls of post offices and railway stations all over the North! The posters offered big rewards for the return of the slaves. And some northern people, too, began to search for us. Black people were stopped on the streets. If they couldn't show a "free pass," they could be thrown into jail and then sent down south.

Many northerners didn't like the Fugitive Slave Law. They didn't want any part of helping southerners get back their slaves. But it wasn't safe anymore for the Underground Railroad to stop in the North. Now it had to run its stations all the way up to Canada!

It also meant that I had to save more money for these trips as a conductor because the Vigilance Committee was no longer paying my way. I had to earn what I needed myself. I took any job I could get—working in hotels, in restaurants, cleaning people's houses, anything. The feeling of being able to earn my own money and pay for what I wanted, that was the sweet taste of freedom itself.

Since my escape I hadn't gone back to the town near my old plantation. I knew, even in my disguise, that I was taking a greater chance at being seen—and recognized! For this trip I dressed as an old woman with a rag tied around my head, a floppy sunhat covering my eyes and a cloth draped over my drooping shoulders. I shuffled my feet as I walked through Bucktown, stopping to buy two chickens, which I carried upside-down.

Glancing around, I caught sight of one of my old masters, Dr. Thompson. He was coming towards me on horseback and suddenly, he looked me straight in the eye! Before he could recognize me, I dropped the birds. They went squawking off across the dusty road. I waved my hands, stooped low and pretended to try to pick them up. Dr. Thompson broke into wild laughter. "Go, old woman, go! Get those chickens!" He passed me by, and I smiled.

"The joke's on you, Master!" I thought.

I hurried to John's cabin and knocked on his door. At first his face froze, and then he became angry. "What are you doing here?" he bellowed. As I started to explain, all excited, another woman came up behind him.

"She's my new wife," he said. "Now go away before you bring trouble on us." The old wooden door slammed in my face. That was the last time I ever saw John Tubman.

A few hours later, I went around to the slave quarters, singing softly:

When that old chariot comes,

> *I'm going to leave you.*
> *I'm bound for the Promised Land,*
> *Friends, I'm going to leave you.*

This time I added:

> *When that old chariot comes,*
> *Who's going with me?*

I heard one reply...then two...then three...

> *When that old chariot comes,*
> *I'm going with you!*

By nightfall I had gotten together a small group of slaves. Every one of them was ready to risk death for the hope of freedom.

Seven days later, Thomas Garrett's carriage stopped just outside the city of Delaware (in the state of Delaware) to let my people out. He motioned towards the path that was well-worn and easy to see. "It will lead you to a wide road," he told them. "You will see signs marking the border between Delaware and Pennsylvania. Step across, and be free!"

I pressed a silver dollar into each person's hand, and they looked at the coins with wonder. This was the first time any of them had ever touched money.

"Godspeed," Mr. Garrett called out, as we watched them go.

I made a lot of freedom trips after that. People

down south began to talk about this anonymous "man" who kept turning up here and there. The masters offered rewards for my capture. And the slaves began to say that, whoever I was, I reminded them of Moses in the Bible, leading his people out of bondage. So that was what they started to call me. Moses became my third name.

Runaway slaves were really free up in Canada. They didn't have to worry about the Fugitive Slave Law. Nobody was going to kidnap them off the streets and take them down south in chains. Blacks in Canada could vote, run for office, send their children to school, and even sit on school boards. You can understand why I decided to rent a house and stay there for a while. Meanwhile, I could work and save money so that I could keep making trips into slave territory, which I did every spring and fall for the next ten years.

One day, I heard that my Papa was about to be arrested for helping a slave escape. The man who told me this said that my father was going to be sent to prison for the rest of his life. That very night, I left for the plantation. Mama cried with happiness when she saw me appear like magic at her cabin door.

On my way there, I had bought a horse from an

old friend. We had built a little wagon out of wooden planks and old wheels that we found lying around. We waited until my Papa came home from the Big House and when it was dark, we set out in the wagon that I had hidden in the woods.

By morning we arrived at a small town. I pulled up to the train station. "Wait here," I told them, and went inside to buy their tickets. While I stood in line, I became aware of two men staring right at me, then glancing at something right above my head. I looked up to see a "Wanted—Dead or Alive" poster with my picture on it. The reward was for ten thousand dollars! I quickly reached over to take a train schedule.

"Oh, it can't be her," one man said to the other. "Tubman can't read or write."

I breathed a sigh of relief, thanking God that I was holding the paper rightside-up.

I got the tickets and gave them to Papa. "Here. Take these fake passes, too. They say your master has given you permission to travel to Wilmington to visit your grandchildren. Get on the train and I'll meet you there."

"Aren't you coming with us?"

With those posters around, I knew I would be a danger to them. "No, you go on ahead. I'll meet

you in Wilmington, and we'll travel to Canada together."

As the train pulled away, I could tell that Mama thought she'd never see me again. But she did!

We all lived together in Saint Catharines, Canada for a while. When the weather got too cold for my folks, we moved to the little town of Auburn, New York. Auburn had been a stop on the Underground, and I knew many people living there. It would be safe for them.

I kept on bringing slaves to freedom, traveling from Maryland into Philadelphia, then to New York City and north through safe houses into Albany, then west to Utica, Syracuse and Rochester and into Canada, until the Civil War broke out in 1861. That was when the northern states and the southern states fought each other. I was sure that a northern victory would mean the end of slavery forever. I wanted to do all I could to help, so when I heard I was needed in Beaufort off the South Carolina coast, I packed my bags and went. Runaways were pouring into that Union-held area, sick and hungry and looking for protection. I acted as a nurse to them and to the wounded soldiers who were brought into the hospital there. I made medicines from roots and herbs, the way my mother had done when I was little.

Many very sick people got better with my medicines.

After President Lincoln signed the Emancipation Proclamation, someone had to go behind enemy lines to tell the slaves that they had been freed. That person had to be someone whom the slaves would believe. The masters were lying to them, telling all kinds of terrible stories so that their slaves would be afraid of the Yankee soldiers and stay far away from them. Of course they didn't want their slaves to know that President Lincoln had said they were now free. So I offered to bring the news secretly into the slave quarters and lead the people from the plantations into Yankee territory where they would be safe. The newly freed men wanted to join the Union army and fight against slavery, but at first, black men weren't allowed into the army. Later that policy was changed, and what brave soldiers they showed themselves to be! Until then I was able to find out all sorts of information from them about the enemy. The information was useful to the Union generals, and that helped the Union army win many battles.

During the war, I was a nurse as well as a spy for the North. I made many secret trips deep into southern territory to find out where the enemy soldiers were camped and what attacks they were planning. I traveled with Colonel Montgomery on a gunboat, calling out to slaves on plantations along the Combahee River to drop their picks and axes and swim to freedom. On one trip we brought more than eight hundred slaves on board! Sometimes I thought it was a miracle that I was never caught or shot.

The war ended in 1865. After almost two hundred-fifty years, the institution of slavery was finally abolished all across the United States. What a glorious day for us all!

After the war, I went to live in Auburn, New York, with my folks, who were old and needed me. I was forty-four years old, and still had much to do. The newly freed people needed money to build schools. And there were so many people, black and white, who were poor and who needed a place to stay and good food to eat. So I planted a garden and sold fruits and vegetables. That way, I made some money to help these people.

A book was written about me, which gave me enough money to buy my house. Now that I owned it, I decided to donate the house to a church so there would always be an open house for anyone who needed a place to stay.

I have seen many things change in my ninety-three years. Slavery in the United States is no more. But many things have remained the same—there is still oppression and poverty. I hope you, my dear reader, will look around you. Stay in touch with your heart. And remember that if you do only one thing at a time, as I did, then you can get a great many things accomplished.

Godspeed.

The Life and Times of
Harriet Tubman

1820   Harriet Tubman is born.

1826   Harriet, now six years old, is hired out.

1849   Harriet escapes to Philadelphia.

1850   The Fugitive Slave Law is passed. Harriet completes her first trip as a conductor on the Underground Railroad.

1851   Harriet makes her first trip with runaways into Canada.

1852   Harriet Beecher Stowe's book *Uncle Tom's Cabin* is published. Many thousands read about the evils of slavery and many begin to speak out against it.

1854   The legend of "Moses" spreads. Reward posters offering up to $40,000 for her—dead or alive—appear in Maryland, Virginia and Delaware.

1857   Harriet rescues her parents from the plantation.

1858   Harriet meets John Brown, a well-known anti-slavery leader.

1859   John Brown tries to get guns at Harper's Ferry (a government arsenal). Brown is captured, tried, and executed.

1860   Abraham Lincoln is elected President of

the United States. The southern states secede from the Union and form the Confederate States of America. Jefferson Davis is elected President of the Confederacy.

1861 The Civil War begins.

1862 Harriet goes to Beaufort to nurse runaways.

1863 President Lincoln signs the Emancipation Proclamation, the famous document that states that all slaves are free. Harriet becomes a spy and a scout for the Union army.

1864 Harriet returns to Auburn, New York.

1865 The Civil War ends. President Lincoln is shot and killed by John Wilkes Booth.

1869 Sarah Hopkins Bradford writes *Scenes in the Life of Harriet Tubman*. With the money Harriet makes from its publication, she purchases her home in Auburn.

1903 Harriet turns her Auburn home over to the African Methodist Episcopal Zion Church of Auburn to be used as a home for the needy.

1913 Harriet Tubman dies in Auburn, New York, at the age of ninety-three.

921
TUB

Polcovar, Jane

Harriet Tubman

$11.93

DATE			
Room 28 Apird 13,			1993
18			
Room 28			
Room T-1			
T-01 — S+			